mel bay presents

christmas solos for beginning viola

level 1

by craig duncan

1 2 3 4 5 6 7 8 9 0

© 1991 BY MEL BAY PUBLICATIONS, INC., PACIFIC, MO.
INTERNATIONAL COPYRIGHT SECURED. ALL RIGHTS RESERVED. PRINTED IN U.S.A.

Contents

These arrangements have been designed to be enjoyed in a number of settings. There are companion books for violin and cello. Each book has the melody and a harmony part, along with piano accompaniment. Suggested uses are:

1. Solo viola with piano accompaniment.

2. Viola duets.

3. Viola and cello duets and trios with the cello book.

4. Viola and violin duets and trios with the violin book.

5. String ensemble using the melody and harmony parts in the violin book, and the harmony parts in the viola and cello books. The cello book can also be played by a bass.

Joy to the World

George Frederick Handel

The First Nowell

English Carol

Angels We Have Heard on High

French Carol

Good King Wenceslas

Traditional Carol

Ding, Dong, Merrily on High

English Carol

The Rocking Carol

English Carol

Once in Royal David's City

English Carol

Silent Night

Franz Gruber 1818

While Shepherds Watched Their Flocks

Traditional

Away in a Manger

Two Traditional Melodies

D.C. al Fine

Jingle Bells

J. Pierpont

14

D. C. al Coda

Coda

Coda

ff

ff

15

O Come, All Ye Faithful

Adeste Fideles

John Francis Wade, 1743

Deck the Halls

English Carol

The Holly and the Ivy

English Carol

Here We Come A-Wassailing

English Carol

We Wish You a Merry Christmas

Traditional Carol